The Christmas Promise

by Lee G. Smith

illustrated by Bill Stroble

Troll Associates

Published by Troll Associates.

Printed in the United States of America.

10 9 8 7 6 5 4 3 2

Rachel Rabbit woke Ted D. Bear and pulled him to the frosty window. She was keeping the promise she had made to him last fall when Ted had said, “Please wake me for Christmas, Rachel. I’ve never seen it—hibernating, you know.”

“Christmas is beautiful,” Ted sighed as the two friends looked out at the fresh snow. Then Ted yawned. “I guess it’s back to bed for me,” he said.

“You can’t go back to bed, Ted,” exclaimed Rachel. “It’s CHRISTMAS! Our friends are waiting for us.”

Ted yawned again. “Why?”

"You'll see. Just come along. But first, put these on. It's cold outside."

"They're very nice," said Ted, taking two knitted things from Rachel. "What are they?"

"It's a scarf and a cap. You can wear them to keep warm. They are my Christmas gifts to you," Rachel said.

"Gifts for Christmas? That's a nice surprise," said Ted. "Thank you." Suddenly Ted did not feel quite so sleepy.

"Merry Christmas!" Nicky Chipmunk called. "We've been waiting for you."

"Where are we going?" shouted Ted.

"To Moose's meadow," said Eliza Ermine.

"Climb aboard."

"Hang on tight!" shouted Nicky as the sled started down, down, down, faster and faster. They swooshed past pine trees and bumped over snow humps.

"Sliiiding downnn a hill cerrrtainly shaaakes meee awaaake," Ted screamed all the way to the bottom.

They slid to a stop at Moose T. Moose's feet. Ted saw his friends rolling snow into a large ball.

"Come help!" they called to Ted.

Ted's friends all agreed it was nice to have a strong bear's help when stacking up the snowballs.

"You finish the snowman, Ted," said Moose.

"Snowman?" Ted said. Then he had an idea. He worked quickly. When he was finished, everyone laughed.

"I thought a snow moose would be nice," Ted said.

"You're very clever, Ted," said Moose. "I'm glad you're with us to celebrate Christmas. Will you help us give out gifts?"

"I'd love to," said Ted.

"Hooray!" everyone shouted.

Ted helped his friends deliver Christmas stockings to the birds. But before hanging the first one on Mr. Feather's branch, Ted discovered something terribly wrong.

"Moose," he whispered, "he'll never be able to wear this sock. It's full of birdseed!"

Moose replied, "Ted, it's a Christmas stocking. The birdseed is Mr. Feather's Christmas present."

"Oh," said Ted. "I didn't think a bird would wear just one sock."

After all the gifts were delivered, Ted helped his friends string Christmas lights. Ted wasn't very good at stringing lights. But he tried hard, and Moose was a good sport about it.

Ted's friends helped him arrange the red berry garland on the Christmas tree.

"Start at the top and work your way down," Mr. Feather directed.

"You need more on the right," said Jenny Goose.

"No, the left," said Ralph Raccoon.

"Oh, please just hurry, Ted!" squealed Fussy Squirrel.

“Please read us a story, Ted,” said Nicky. Ted opened the book Nicky handed him. His friends gathered around to listen to him read a Christmas story.

When he finished reading, Ted told everyone to follow him outside. "Merry Christmas!" he shouted. Then he passed out presents to everyone—crunchy acorns, juicy berries, sweet honey, and other tasty treats. Ted gave a special gift to Rachel and said, "Thank you for keeping your promise, Rachel. I've had a wonderful Christmas."

"You're welcome," Rachel said. "But Christmas isn't over yet. Follow me!"

Rachel and her friends brought Ted to his mailbox. Ted's mailbox never, ever had anything in it for Christmas. But today it was stuffed with packages and cards from all the forest animals.

Ted and his friends had fun all day long. When darkness fell, they admired the bright stars in the sky above them.

"I'll remember this Christmas always," sighed Ted. Everyone agreed they would, too.

Suddenly a shooting star blazed across the sky. Before it burned out of sight, Ted said, "I wish I could spend many more Christmases with my friends."

"You will," Rachel said. "We'll wake you up again next year."

"Promise?" Ted asked. All his friends answered, "We promise, Ted. Merry Christmas!"